CASE STUDIES IN EDUCATION:
A COMMONWEALTH VIEW

Providing Education for Out-of-School Youth in Bangladesh

Muhammad Ibrahim

Commonwealth Secretariat

Published by:

Commonwealth Secretariat

Marlborough House
Pall Mall
London SW1Y 5HX
United Kingdom

© Commonwealth Secretariat, 2002

Designed by Allard & Gan design

Further copies may be purchased from:
Publications Unit Commonwealth Secretariat
Telephone: +44 (0)20 7747 6342
Facsimile: +44 (0)20 7839 9081
Web site: http//www. thecommonwealth.org

ISBN 0-85092-690-4

Price: £5.99

Printed by Formara Limited

Contents

Acronyms

ABS	Advanced Basic School
AGP	Adolescent Girls' Programme
BEOC	Basic Education for Older Children
BRAC	Bangladesh Rural Advancement Committee
BS	Basic School
BSS	Basic School System
CAMPE	Campaign for Popular Education
CBA	Centre Based Approach
CMES	Centre for Mass Education in Science
DAM	Dhaka Ahsania Mission
DNFE	Directorate of Non-Formal Education
FIVDB	Friends in Village Development in Bangladesh
GEP	General Education Project
GSS	Gono Shahajjo Shongstha
IDEAL	Intensive District Approach to Education for All
INFEP	Integrated Non-Formal Education Project
NFE	Non-Formal Education
NFPE	Non-Formal Primary Education
NGO	Non-Governmental Organisation
PMED	Primary and Mass Education Division
R & D	Research and Development
RTC	Rural Technology Centre
TLM	Total Literacy Movement
UCEP	Underprivileged Children's Education Programme
UN	United Nations
UO	Unit Organiser
VTI	Vocational Training Institute

Executive Summary

In 1995 the literacy rate in Bangladesh was set at 44.30 per cent. However, in recent years the enrolment rate in primary schools has increased and has now reached about 90 per cent. But the dropout rate is still too high; more than half of those enrolled drop out before completing their primary education, most with little educational competency. They form a very big group of out-of-school youth who need a second chance for education.

The marginalised population, which has the most propensity for non-enrolment and dropping out, has been served through Non-Formal Education (NFE). This approach adopts different strategies and provides various flexibilities within basic or primary education, so that target groups can be reached. Many Non-Governmental Organisations (NGOs) in Bangladesh have participated in NFE programmes, some with quite effective, innovative models. These took the form of feeder schools to the formal stream, full Non-Formal Primary Education (NFPE), or NFE for adolescents and adults. More recently, since the 1990s, the Government of Bangladesh has taken up major NFE programmes of its own. A Directorate for Non-Formal Education (DNFE) has been entrusted with the task. In its Centre Based Approach (CBA), DNFE has organised nine-month literacy programmes for adolescents and adults implemented through NGOs. DNFE's Total Literacy Movement (TLM), a campaign-type intervention under the local administration, mobilises efforts to establish literacy centres for nine months and to reach all those who are illiterate.

While the NGOs work in NFE mainly with their target groups whom they serve with various development efforts, the government programmes have to cover vast numbers of target groups in a short space of time. NGOs can therefore afford to approach the problem more professionally, stressing completeness, quality, application and linkages of education in NFE. The government, on the other hand, offers only literacy courses. The post-literacy and continuing education arrangements for NFE are still in an unsatisfactory state, though NGOs have rather more substantial programmes for these.

While there are many reasons for such a vast number of out-of-school youth(unenrolled or dropouts) these can be summarised as follows:

- dependence on the youth's income, (opportunity cost);

- a feeling of the irrelevance of education in their lives, and

- gender discrimination.

[handwritten: the same as Africa! (+ US, UK)]

The key to an effective second chance education for these young people is in addressing the causes, especially by integrating education with their livelihood efforts. Most of the existing NFE programmes, both in the government and the NGO sectors, are not designed to address these causes specifically. DNFE offers only literacy. Though NGOs offer more, most of them stop short of addressing real life adolescent issues, for example the acquisition of technical skills leading to immediate income generation,and the involvement of young people in activities to eliminate gender discrimination.

[handwritten: very interesting]

There are, however, some successful efforts that have fully addressed these problems and have a good potential for replication. This study has identified two such efforts, the Centre for Mass Education in Science (CMES) programme and the Underprivileged Children's Education Programme (UCEP), because of their bold innovative approaches. Other programmes, for example, Bangladesh Rural Advancement Committee (BRAC), Basic Education for Older Children (BEOC) and the Dhaka Ahsania Mission (DAM), Gonokendra model, have also been identified for the case study, as they too are effective models for attracting out-of-school youth, though they do not specifically involve themselves with livelihood activities.

CMES has developed its Basic School System (BSS) to offer an integrated education package to out-of-school youth, comprising general education up to lower secondary level, technology skills training and practice for income-generation, and "home-to-home work" in health and the environment. A unit, a cluster of its Basic Schools (BSs), Advanced Basic Schools (ABSs) and the Rural Technology Centre (RTC), does the job. The general education and technical components interact closely to make both richer in quality and relevance to everyday life. The technology practice takes place at market level, thus providing an immediate income to the target group. The CMES Adolescent Girls' Programme (AGP), an action-oriented programme for the empowerment of girls, has proved to be a very powerful supportive programme to BSS. Programmes for continuing education and graduate work have also been very supportive with regard to the objective of providing a meaningful second chance education to out-of-school youth. The whole course up to the equivalent of Grade VIII should take five years.

The UCEP programme organises NFE schools for the general education of employed urban adolescents and youth, offering up to Grade VIII within four-and-a-half years. Some students are selected for UCEP's "technical" schools, which offer trade courses lasting from six months to two years, while others are accommodated in UCEP's "para-trade" centres to be trained in simpler trades. Three different shifts in the "general" schools give working children a choice of times so that their existing work, so important for their survival, may be continued. Though courses are condensed, the quality of education, and regular attendance and progress are emphasised. The UCEP Employment Programme takes up initiatives so that almost all the graduates of technical education and most of the graduates of general education get suitable employment with higher income and potential than before.

BRAC's intervention in this field comes through its BEOC programme. It is a three-year schooling programme, covering the whole of the primary curriculum in a condensed form. A life-oriented curriculum, and materials appropriate for adolescents are its specific characteristics. The curriculum includes some supplementary subjects dealing with life skills. The much tested and replicated BRAC methods of quality education and education-monitoring have been applied in this case, too. BRAC's continuing education programme through its library schemes has also indirectly contributed to the education of this target group.

DAM's Gonokendra (People's Centre) model is a grassroots library with facilities for entertainment and social interaction. A variety of appropriate reading materials can be used for study, discussion and training. DAM facilitators and community workers help in the process, while supervisors monitor progress. The curriculum can be applied in accordance with the participants' needs. The level is designed for the newly literate youth and adults, and self-motivated learning is emphasised. The community plays a major role in organising Gonokendra and will ultimately take charge of it.

1. An Overview of the NFE Situation in Bangladesh

Basic and Primary Education in Bangladesh

The Literacy and Enrolment Situation

According to the Bangladesh Bureau of Statistics, the literacy rate of the age 7+ population in 1995 was 44.30 per cent. Of this, the male literacy rate was 50.40 per cent and the female literacy rate, 28.50 per cent. In a 123 million population with a 7+ aged population of 100 million, 55 million are illiterate, of whom 37 million are female. According to a 1996 estimate of the Planning Commission of Bangladesh, the primary school-aged population was 17.519 million. Enrolment came to 89.64 per cent of this figure, and improved to 92 per cent if NGO non-formal schools were included.

The Education Watch Report 1998, an independent attempt by a research group to assess the primary education situation in Bangladesh on a yearly basis, surveyed 312 villages from all 64 districts and the metropolitan cities and arrived at a weighted national net enrolment rate of 77 per cent for 1998. This means that 23 per cent of children, 6-10 years of age, were not enrolled. Girls' enrolment was actually more (78.6 per cent) than boys' (75.5 per cent). An analysis of the gross enrolment information showed that one-third of all students enrolled in primary classes came from above the primary age group (6-10 years).

In spite of these gaps, the progress in enrolment during recent years, roughly over a decade, has been phenomenal. Efforts were supported by social mobilisation campaigns, building more schools, establishing feeder schools, introducing a more highly developed primary school curriculum and recruiting a greater number of female teachers into the system. Bangladesh now has nearly 80,000 schools providing primary education. On average, there is a primary school for every 1.85 square kilometres.

Various Realities in Primary Education

Primary schools have five classes, Grade I to Grade V. Lack of space and teachers causes the classes to be conducted in a staggered manner, in two shifts with Grades I and II meeting from 10.00 a.m. to 12.00 p.m. and Grades III-V from 12.15 p.m to 16.15 p.m.

About 83 per cent of enrolled students attend government primary schools, the rest go to private schools of various kinds or to madrassas (religious schools) at the primary level. The registered private primary schools receive some financial support from the government. Like the government primary schools, education here is free for the students and so are the textbooks which are based on the National Curriculum.

According to the Education Watch Report for 1998, the dropout rate varied from 4 to 7 per cent and the repeater rate from 4 to 11 per cent for various classes. The national primary school dropout rate was estimated to be 55.8 per cent for girls and 59.2 per cent for boys. Absenteeism has been found to be quite high, with 59 per cent of students in school on a typical day (the day of visit by the survey team). As for the basic literacy and numeracy competencies achieved, 7.5 per cent of children completing one year of schooling satisfied the minimum level. The figures are 20.8 per cent for those completing three years, and 56.9 per cent for those completing five years. Though this shows significant progress compared with a similar test in 1993, the quality of education has not kept pace with the progress in enrolment. The retention rate and the attendance rate also remained stagnant.

The Educational Aims, Policies and Programmes in Formal Primary Education

The 1990 World Conference on Education for All and World Summit for Children had a profound impact on the primary and basic education policies in Bangladesh. The Constitution of the country enshrines the right of the child to free and compulsory primary education. This obliges the government to adopt effective measures for:

- establishing a uniform, providing a mass-oriented and universal system of education, and extending free and compulsory education to all children to such a stage as may be determined by law;

- relating education to the needs of the society and producing properly trained and motivated citizens to serve these needs; and

- eradicating illiteracy within such time as may be determined by law.

The goal of the Government of Bangladesh in the primary education sector is to provide all primary school-aged children (6-10 years) with access to quality primary education and an environment sufficient to encourage them to attend school regularly and to successfully complete a five-year primary education cycle.

The following policy and programme follow-up of these principles took place from 1990 onwards:

(a) The Primary Education (Compulsory) Act was passed by Parliament in 1990.

(b) A new, competency-based curriculum was introduced in primary schools, beginning with Grade I in 1992 and finishing with Grade V in 1996.

(c) A Primary and Mass Education Division (PMED) was created within the Ministry of Education in 1992 to provide administrative support to policies and programmes for the universalisation of primary education and the eradication of illiteracy.

(d) A multi-faceted five-year General Education Project (GEP) was implemented (1992-96) for the improvement of primary level education.

(e) As a successor to GEP, another programme, entitled Primary Education Development Programme, geared to improve access/enrolment, attendance, completion, supervision and management has been launched (1997).

(f) A number of experiments are in progress in various IDEAL (Intensive District Approach to Education for All) districts, to improve teachers' school management through intensive community participation. These also include school mapping and the identification of school-aged children, family contacts for reducing absenteeism and dropouts, local level planning, and school attractiveness programmes.

The Role Played by NFE (Basic and Primary)

The Nature of NFE

In spite of all the progress in formal primary education in recent years, the marginalised population still remains out of reach, either due to non-enrolment or to dropping out early. The role of Non-Formal Education (NFE) comes into its own here. NFE has the flexibilities required for overcoming the barriers for these target groups, which the formal system does not have.

The flexibilities include those of age, space, hours, teachers (e.g. community teachers), dress, routine, methods, materials and curriculum. NFE can organise education more in keeping with the livelihood of the students and their families, and may include life skills and even income-generating activities to reduce the opportunity costs for the students. It may provide not only free textbooks, but also other basic essentials for learning such as workbooks, pencils, etc., thereby reducing private costs. Most of all, NFE is more community-oriented, with the community directly participating in the organisation and management of education. In short, NFE can formulate its own strategies to reach those normally out of reach and to retain them within education long enough to have the practical benefits.

[handwritten margin note: but formal can change these!!]

Approaches to NFE by NGOs

NFE in Bangladesh has been basically an NGO domain. Long before the government's Education For All programme started, various NGOs had been conducting NFE programmes as a part of their development efforts with the marginalised target groups. Some of these had been already quite innovative and effective. A recent independent survey has concluded that though there are many NGOs involved in the delivery of NFE programmes, only a few are important players as they advocate new models, provide curriculum materials and have established networks under partnerships. The survey has mentioned the following as the important players in NFE: BRAC, PROSHIKA, Gono Shahajjo Shongstha (GSS), Nijera Shikhi, Dhaka Ahsania Mission (DAM), Friends in Village Development in Bangladesh (FIVDB), Action Aid, Centre for Mass Education in Science (CMES) and the Underprivileged Children's Education Programme (UCEP).

In general, NFE took the following courses of action:

(i) **Feeder schools for formal primary education:** These are schools providing the few early years of education for the primary school-aged group, in a convenient location, in a non-formal setting with the objective of subsequently sending the learners to a formal school. The BRAC programme has been the biggest and most famous example of this system. Many other NGOs also adopted the BRAC model. In this model a teacher in one school takes the same group of students from Grade I to Grade III in three years, then they are enrolled in Grade IV in a formal primary school. There is a monitoring and supervision arrangement within the model.

(ii) **Full Non-Formal Primary Education (NFPE):** There have been some NGO programmes which cater for the whole primary education school system from Grade I to Grade V. Naturally, there are more flexibilities in age for the students here, and many of them tend to be older than the usual primary school-aged student.

(iii) **NFE for adolescents and adults:** This has been dispensed through so-called Mass Education Centres which deal with basic literacy and numeracy for illiterate adolescents and adults. Many NGOs have organised this form of NFE for their target group families. They have usually offered it as a part of their general development efforts. A Mass Education Centre usually has a teacher who conducts a class of a mixed group of adolescents and adults for one to two hours in a convenient location. The aims and achievements have varied: from the ability to sign one's name to a reasonable competency of reading and writing, up to being able to read or write a letter. There are separate classes for female and male learners. But the female learners usually predominate, as they are more likely to be available in the homestead area during the daytime, while male learners can make time only at night, if at all.

iv) **Basic and primary education for adolescents along with skills training for livelihood:** Only a few NGOs have pioneered this approach, targeting mainly adolescent dropouts and working children. Their efforts have been very innovative and the models they created have received more and more attention in a wide arena recently. Emphasis has been placed on the need to connect work and employment opportunities with NFE for the above target groups.

Government Policies and Efforts in NFE

As part of its drive towards Education For All, the Government of Bangladesh initiated a NFE project in 1991 called INFEP (Integrated Non-Formal Education Project).

This had four components:

(i)   pre-primary education for 4-5 year olds;

(ii) basic education (NFPE) for 6-10 year olds;

(iii) adolescent education for 11-14 year olds; and

(iv) adult education for those 15 to 45 years old.

The project was implemented mainly through participating NGOs during 1993-96. A total of 1,791,497 children and 734,498 adults were registered in the project in 1996. At about the same time, the government's General Education Project (GEP) had a small NFE component which was implemented through participating NGOs. This dealt with non-formal primary education for the 6-14 age group, either through feeder schools or through full non-formal primary schools.

The INFEP experience led the government to establish a Directorate for Non-Formal Education (DNFE) under the Primary and Mass Education Division of the Ministry of Education, which took over the INFEP task from 1996. The DNFE has adopted three modalities of delivery for NFE, namely the Centre Based Approach (CBA), the Total Literacy Movement (TLM) and the Book Distribution Model (BDM).

Centre Based Approach (CBA)

DNFE organised this nine-month literacy programme for adolescents and adults, contracting NGOs to implement the programme in various areas of the country. DNFE provides financial support, primers, curriculum materials, teacher and supervisor training to the NGOs. Lately, a three-month post-literacy phase has been added, allowing learners increased access to reading materials. DNFE has appointed a District Co-ordinating Officer (DCO) and monitoring associates to co-ordinate and monitor the programme. It also brings in local civil administration and community leaders to assist in these efforts.

Centre Based Approach (CBA) and the other modalities of DNFE, have been implemented in several phases. These phases are referred to as NFE-1, NFE-2, NFE-3, NFE-4. Within NFE-1 CBA, 0.18 million learners were reached by mid-1998. A further 0.4 million learners were reached through CBA in NFE-2.

CBA in NFE-3 has a different target group, 8-10 year old, urban, working children, and the programme has been named Hard to Reach. This, too, was implemented by NGOs working in urban areas.

Total Literacy Movement (TLM)

This is a campaign model under the leadership of the District Commissioner (DC), the chief administrative officer in a district, who mobilises the district administration, institutions and the political system for the cause. The administration assigns a government officer for a smaller administrative unit to take responsibility for the survey, the establishment of centres, the appointment of teachers and supervisors, and the implementation of the programme. The training offered for teachers and supervisors is the same as in CBA. As there are many volunteers who offer their services free, the per learner unit cost of Total Literacy Movement (TLM) is half of that incurred in CBA. The learning period is nine months with a post-literacy phase of three months.

In NFE-1 some 180,000 illiterates achieved literacy, and 1.45 million in NFE-2. NFE-4 uses only the TLM approach and targets 22.8 million learners.

Book Distribution Model

Here DNFE provides books and other literacy materials to some local voluntary organisations who arrange the learning centres for illiterate adolescents and adults.

A Critical Analysis of Current Trends in NFE

GO and NGO Approaches

NFE used to be a predominantly NGO activity in Bangladesh. But with the creation of DNFE and its various programmes, the government has also become a major player in the field. In the CBA approach, DNFE depends on NGOs for the implementation, while in the TLM approach it depends on the administration.

In spite of the fact that a part of the DNFE programme is actually being implemented by NGOs, there are broad differences between NGO and GO (Government Organisation) approaches to NFE. NGO programmes usually have an integrated approach, taking up education along with other empowerment inputs, such as savings groups, micro-credit, skills training, health programmes, gender awareness, etc. Their main emphasis in education is on the children of the target group families, while the adults themselves come into it only as part of the total empowerment programme. In both cases the NGOs can stress quality rather than quantity. They can afford to arrange longer term and more intensive programmes – being concerned about issues such as relevance to real life, the learner-centred approach and the participatory nature of the class, including feedback from the learners. They are also concerned with gender awareness, continuous evaluation, strategies for ensuring attendance, the content and application of literacy, and a more effective post-literacy programme, etc.

The government programme, on the other hand, has to be delivered quickly, covering a vast number of people within a very specific, short space of time. It is caught between an ambitious goal determined by the political agenda of a democratic government and the bureaucratic apparatus limited by the rules and regulations and the style of work of such apparatus. Even when NGOs are involved in the implementation, they have to operate under those limitations. Nine months is a short time while government machinery has to keep pace with the various steps of the programme, and much can lag behind by the time the pre-arranged moment of graduation arrives.

However, the GO approach is remarkable in its coverage and perhaps something like this is inevitable if the much needed eradication of illiteracy has to be achieved within a stipulated time. DNFE places emphasis on the TLM mode rather than that of the CBA, precisely for this reason. For example, NFE-4, a much bigger project than the earlier ones, aims to reach 22.8 million learners entirely through the TLM approach. This shows that the trend is to depend on the campaign model based on administrative machinery and volunteers, rather than on the more professional, slower approach of the NGOs.

There is also a general difference between the objectives of NGO efforts and GO efforts. The major NGO/NFE programmes concentrate on the primary education of disadvantaged children and adolescents. This has a more highly developed curriculum similar to the National Primary Curriculum, albeit a more life-oriented one, and goes beyond acquiring literacy and numeracy. On the other hand, the DNFE programme aims at the mass eradication of illiteracy within a wide range of age groups through a short intervention.

Flexibility within NFE

The essence of NFE is its flexibility to address the diverse target groups which need it, and this is how NFE was being dispensed by various NGOs. But the trend now is to conduct totally uniform and specified programmes under a centralised authority (DNFE). As opposed to the programmes for appropriate education that NGOs innovated for their target groups, these are pure literacy programmes. It can hardly be expected that illiterate adolescents and adults attending a learning centre for one to two hours a day for nine months, with frequent absenteeism, will reach a level of literacy that will be retained. There is no scope for simultaneous practices and associations with other educative activities that would have reinforced the process.

It is those practices, associations and other activities which necessitate a flexibility in curriculum, methods and materials. Although NGOs are being employed to implement the government programme in the case of CBA, and some of these NGOs are very innovative in NFE strategies in their own programmes, they have little autonomy of their own. The same books, strict schedules, rules and regulations have to be followed literally by everyone. This means that the activities can be monitored quickly, but it does not improve the results. As most of the NFE programmes are now diverted from being NGO programmes to being DNFE programmes, and donor support concentrates on the latter, NFE is in real danger of losing its essence – the flexibility which enables it to reach those who are out of reach.

It must be admitted that this loss of flexibility did not start overnight with the intervention of the government. The process started earlier within the NGO programmes themselves, at least within many of them. In the interest of easy replication, there had been a tendency to customise their education packages, so that NFE could bear an increasing resemblance to mainstream education. The emphasis on being the feeders into the formal schools also necessitated such an approach. The claims of speciality made by these NGO/NFE schools were not so much because of their appropriateness to the target group, but more for their quality of education. What tended to be forgotten in the process was that given the disadvantaged nature of the target group, they might need a whole different education stream commensurate with their livelihood obligations. This required radically different educational strategies, which only a few of the NGOs attempted to provide. *paradigm shift !*

Post-Literacy and Continuing Education.

The fact that pure literacy programmes cannot sustain their effectiveness without reinforcement is certainly recognised. But there has not yet been any satisfactory answer to this problem. In the DNFE programmes, post-literacy is taken care of by providing access to more reading materials for another three months. This, obviously, is a poor substitute for continuing education, the more so because the mechanism which will provide the learners with opportunities and increase motivation, is poorly organised and not well-defined

Some NGOs in their own programmes try to address the problem by trying to introduce an element of stability, e.g. organising permanent libraries or reading centres for their graduates. The fact that these are permanent arrangements for NFE graduates, that the extent of education previously imparted is usually not limited to literacy, and that the target group concerned has other activity-oriented relationships with the NGOs, gives this kind of approach a better chance of success. Some NGOs can even organise study circles and training sessions in these libraries, sometimes with the help of a facilitator. The problem here is a motivational one. Those graduates of NFE who are not mainstreamed (mostly adolescents and adults) would be absorbed in their livelihood struggles and domestic chores in the days that follow. An arrangement which does not address these livelihood and economic needs would not have sufficient attraction for them.

An increasingly sustained approach to continuing education would need more substantial action and activities concerning their livelihood, along with the practice of literacy. For example, peer-organised social action relating to gender issues and issues concerning improvement in skills and incomes has been found to form a better basis for continuing education for NFE graduates.

2. Educational Programmes for the Out-of-school Youth of Bangladesh

Out-of-school Youth and Reasons for Exclusion

Who Are the Out-of-school Youth?

In recent years, enrolment in primary education has increased. But even so, more than 20 per cent of primary school-aged children still remain unenrolled. Moreover, the retention rate has not followed the improvement in enrolment. The rate of dropping out before finishing all primary school classes stands higher than 50 per cent. A huge number of children therefore enter their adolescence out of school, either as unenrolled or as dropouts. Whatever they had learned in school they usually fail to retain, and most of them do not have a second chance at education. So there are millions of young people who have not acquired the basic competencies of literacy and numeracy. The Education Watch Survey for 1998 has shown that less than one-third enter their adolescence with any meaningful learning. The remainder is a large proportion.

Reasons for Exclusion

When we consider the reasons and circumstances under which these adolescents dropped out, or did not enrol in the first place, abject poverty is the probable cause in most cases. The opportunity-cost of remaining in school is too high for them. For many poor families, a boy or a girl is already economically indispensable, as soon as he/she is 7-8 years old. Late enrolment and the frequent repetition of primary school classes make young people even older and therefore even more indispensable, while still in school. The long, hard journey through school and college, which is required before any tangible effect of education can be related to life, is just too long for them.

In NGO surveys conducted so that they can persuade adolescents and their parents to enrol young people in their NFE programmes, various situations

13

affecting dropouts are faced. Every one of them has a story to tell – whether he/she is a recent dropout, a 10-year-old, or someone in his/her teens, already absorbed in an area other than education.

The stories revolve around the following reasons:

- Parents need their assistance at work.

- Some essential income for the family depends on them.

- The family cannot bear the real costs associated with education.

- The school is too far away for the girl to travel safely. She is grown up now, and cannot continue.

- Some tempting local opportunities for income which the family cannot do without, e.g. catching shrimp spawn, tending mango gardens.

- Earning losses are the obvious reasons which are highlighted. But there are also other more subtle reasons.

One such reason is a crisis of relevance. Many children from poor families come to feel that they gain nothing continuing their education. They lose confidence in overcrowded classes, feeling neglected and failing to achieve much there. They feel more and more that school is for those who would be able to continue through secondary level and beyond, and they are not among this group. It is never emphasised that education as a whole may be useful, and is valuable in its own right. So, relieved from the burdens of school, they try in contrast, to prove their worth out of school – in being economically helpful to the family.

Gender discrimination against girls in rural society is also a reason for adolescent dropouts. It is still not uncommon to treat girls differently as soon as they reach puberty. Many parents do not like the idea of letting them mix with outsiders any more, and think that to let them continue at school brings extra complications. Girls are, after all, regarded as a burden by many parents who will need expensive dowries when they marry.

What are They Doing out of School?

As we can guess, young people who drop out of school are busy being economically useful. But this is not always the case. Many of them are only marginally involved in economic activity, while others may add significantly to the family income.

Families are often so poor however, that children's contributions, however marginal are vital. These can take the form of giving domestic help to parents, looking after cattle, occasionally tending the kitchen garden, or running errands. With boys, there might be free time to while away at the bazaar or tea stall. Some of these idle brains may find undesirable means of spending time, such as teasing girls or gossiping.

For those boys who may be involved in serious economic activities, these activities would mostly involve unskilled labour: agricultural labour, rickshaw pulling, marketing family produce etc. Employment for cash income is not easily available for dropouts.

Adolescent girls mainly help their mothers in the kitchen and in other activities, such as crop processing, and raising younger siblings. Some girls work as domestic servants or in home-based production. Some may even find their way to the city to work in garment factories or other industries. For many out-of-school adolescent girls there is not a great deal of useful activity. They are just waiting to be married off as soon as possible.

The Problems and Scope for the Education of Out-of-school Youth.

The Nature of the Problems

The nature of the problem of education for out-of-school youth does not just involve the question of access to education, nor even the quality of education in the usual sense. It also involves the availability of an education appropriate for this target group. The original causes for their dropping out or for their non-enrolment do not vanish if a second chance for education is offered to them. All the causes: the opportunity cost, the fear of irrelevance, the gender issues, still remain effective. Any educational effort for them which neglects to address these basic realities would not succeed.

In addressing these realities the following aspects have to be borne in mind:

- The opportunity to continue and improve upon income-generating activities essential to the family;

- Immediate opportunity for the implementation of improved literacy, numeracy and life skills acquired through education;

- An educational atmosphere in which he/she can bring in his/her own life issues and participate fully; attaining competencies quickly and effectively;

- An education which provides guidance and assistance in his/her real life including improved quality of life and employment;

- A liberating atmosphere gender-wise which releases girls from some of the discriminating pressures, especially those of early marriage and confinement.

Obviously, the education of out-of-school youth involves more aspects that have to be considered than when involved in a straightforward education dealing simply with literacy. Then comes the question of diversity. There is a common link among all dropout adolescents, in that they are all disadvantaged. However, they are disadvantaged in different ways. For many of them, it is poverty which comes foremost. But this is not the case for everyone. For some, poverty is not extreme, rather it is the feeling of alienation from the existing school which comes foremost. Parents' indifference, and in some cases, outright discouragement, is involved in many cases. Broken homes, divorced or abandoned mothers for example are at the heart of much educational discontinuity. And of course, gender discrimination has to be considered. Second chance education for out-of-school youth will somehow have to redress these disadvantages so diversely caused. Unless it attempts to do this, the underlying causes of lack of education will continue to be there in this phase too, rendering it ineffective or too short-lived.

The Scope for a Second Chance

There is certainly scope for organising education for out-of-school youth, although this will be quite challenging. The key is to inspire young people with new hope, enabling them to stand on their own feet, and equipping them with usable skills. Inviting adolescents and adults to join the literacy centres for nine months can hardly achieve this. The question is not simply one of literacy, but that of an appropriate education.

The expectations of out-of-school youth brought back into education relate directly to the world of work. This demands vocational training, income-generating activities and credit. The scope for integrating these with education opens up the possibilities for a second chance for out-of-school youth. Some NGOs in Bangladesh have realised this in their successful NFE initiatives, and there is no reason why these cannot be replicated for the needs of this huge group – out-of-school youth. For an adolescent dropout, the changeover from a working boy/girl to a student has to be a smooth one. It usually does not help to keep their study and the vocational part of their education in two different compartments. So, rather unconventionally, one has to mix the two. The biggest advantage to such a strategy is the feeling that there is no barrier between the working world and the educational world. They earn as they learn.

Similarly, the scope is widened even further when the adolescent girl or young woman is helped to overcome the barriers of gender discrimination and stereotyping within this education. It is this opportunity for a new way of thinking, exploiting their potential, that can attract them to an effective education, in spite of their past and present disadvantages in life.

Existing Mainstream Policies and Programmes

NFE Organised by DNFE

By far the most significant programme in NFE now belongs to DNFE, and most of the resources from the international donors as well as the government, are concentrated on the DNFE programmes. But there is no specific place for the education of out-of-school youth in this programme. Out-of-school-youth are included with all other 'illiterates' for whose literacy the DNFE programmes (both CBA and TLM) are organised. The age range for these programmes is very broad, 11-45 years and the approach is a uniform one of pure literacy. This does not include education beyond literacy, nor does it include any linkage with the broader issue of livelihood.

Obviously as far as out-of-school youth are concerned, this is a poor substitute for an appropriate second chance education, and it is unlikely to have much sustainable effect. The government realises the need for continuing education with the necessary linkages. But it has scarcely explored all the possibilities. Even the models available within the country in the NGO sector have not really been examined. Rather DNFE's NFE-4 consists entirely of TLM, the 'only literacy approach' targeted to reach 22.8 million learners through a campaign led by the administration.

The Role of the Vocational Education Sector

The opportunities for technical and vocational education in Bangladesh remain very limited. Most institutional arrangements for this need at least a high school graduation (e.g. polytechnics, commercial institutes). However, there are Vocational Training Institutes (VTIs) which need a high school education equivalent to only Grade VIII. But as most dropping out from school takes place much earlier than that, the majority of out-of-school youth cannot take advantage of this opportunity.

In fact, the admission criteria and other formal aspects of VTIs, discourage many who would really benefit from them, in the sense that they badly need hands-on income-generating skills for their livelihood. The reality is that well-equipped and capital intensive arrangements in VTIs often remain underutilised, and the enrolled, more often than not, come from comparatively well-off families who ultimately do not soil their hands with manual work. The intake of all government technical and vocational institutes combined (164 of them) including VTIs, polytechnics, commercial institutes and other assorted technical and engineering institutes, consists of only 43,635 students, 3,630 of them female.

Outside the government-run institutes, there are some private trade schools, mainly in cities and towns. Most of these are run on commercial lines, though there are some sponsored by NGOs and charitable organisations. Influenced by the VTIs and the predominant employment criteria, they also tend to require a high school education of at least Grade VIII. Few of these schools, however, include general education in their curriculum. As a result, school dropouts cannot have a second chance education here, nor can they proceed with the vocational part because of the admission criteria.

The limitations of the vocational education sector, and its reduced relevance to out-of-school youth, have lately come to the attention of the policymakers in this sector. The Bangladesh Technical Education Board is now coming up with a plan for a flexible mode of technical education combined with general education, which can be dispensed in a more informal way. This will be specially targeted at dropout adolescents and will try to build upon the abilities of young people who are working. This would identify the needs of dropout adolescents and prepare a curriculum of general and vocational education appropriate for them. The admission criteria will be flexible and will also take account of their work-experience as Prior Learning Experience (PLE). The general education part of this plan will be entrusted to the selected high schools of the locality. This plan is the first serious attempt on the part of the government education policy to focus on appropriate education for out-of-school youth, although the actual mode of implementation is still unclear.

The Role of NGOs.

The major practitioners of NFE, the NGOs, usually have an arrangement for adolescent education: for those who are beyond primary school age, but still need a basic and primary education. But more often than not, this is basically a repeat of the same curriculum and methods that are used for younger children. The differences at best consist of some more life-oriented subjects within the textbooks such as gender equity, democratic practices, etc. Only in a minority of the cases is there an attempt to address the other real life adolescent issues including those of livelihood or technical skills.

Some NGOs can still manage to achieve satisfactory enrolment and attendance, because of their involvement with the students' families in other programmes such as micro-credit, marketing channels, etc., even if those do not directly involve young people. For others, the adolescent part of NFE is always the weaker part, because unlike the primary school-aged children, they do not have the necessary incentives; and most of the reasons for their non-enrolment or dropping out still remain unaddressed.

There are also other NGOs which have faced up to the problems of out-of-school youth These NGOs at least do not assume that the problems will go away as soon as a school for adolescents is made available. These are the ones who choose their strategies according to their target group, whether they are urban, working children, garment worker girls who have just lost their jobs, or rural, unemployed youth trying to be useful to their farm labourer parents. These NGOs try to provide a new outlet for them, through education and skills-training, making it worth their while even when they are receiving education. These are the NGOs who have achieved success in addressing this very important area in the field of education in Bangladesh, an area which is by and large neglected by most of the major players in NFE.

3. Case Studies Indicating Successful NFE Initiatives for Out-of-school Youth

Selection Criteria

A range of interventions exists for the education of out-of-school young people in Bangladesh. The government programme for this group is not a specific one. Rather, it is a part of the nine-month basic literacy programme for adolescents and adults. Many of the NGO programmes including some large ones, arrange for schooling specific to this adolescent group, and offer a fuller curriculum package leading towards an informal primary education. The content of the curriculum often tries to include discussion of some of the life skills in its supplementary material, e.g. health, family environment and gender equality. The various criteria for a quality education are considered in the best of these arrangements, such as student participation, receptivity and recreational needs, teacher quality, supervision and management, etc. These factors definitely add to the educational achievements and to the success of enrolment and retention.

But of these NGO efforts only a few have tried to address the basic issues of opportunity: cost, unemployment, feeling of irrelevance, gender discrimination, and lack of empowerment etc., which have kept this group out of school. Few have introduced effective innovations within their second chance schooling in order to overcome these barriers. We feel that these are the types of intervention which deserve more attention, in order to improve the design and delivery of effective education for out-of-school youth. In this category we have selected the CMES and UCEP programmes to consider as case studies.

However, other efforts, while not being as proactive in overcoming the barriers mentioned earlier, have been successful models for adolescent NFE in Bangladesh, because of their improved methods, and materials designed to suit the target group and to impart a quality education. The BRAC programme has been the largest and most representative of this group. DAM (Dhaka Ahsania Mission) has been conducting a rather different continuing education programme based on "'people's centres" where young people can participate in flexible, self-motivated studies based around a library. Shorter discussions of the BRAC and DAM programmes are therefore also included as case studies.

The CMES Programme

The Target Group

The Centre for Mass Education in Science (CMES) was established in 1978 with the objective of taking the benefits of science and technology to the grassroots for the common people of Bangladesh. It made practically oriented mass education its major objective.

Human resource development is an urgent need in Bangladesh, and potentially its most fruitful investment. It has to come through universal education and livelihood skills. Unfortunately, a very large group of unenrolled and dropout adolescents remains outside these parameters, and contributes to society's increasing frustration and bewilderment. CMES has targeted this group, especially those from poor, rural families.

The CMES experience with adolescent dropouts from disadvantaged families shows that most of them have had little schooling. Even those who claim to have attended up to Grade IV or V, scarcely achieve basic literacy. Typically they come from landless farmlabourer families who have little other than their meagre homesteads. Some may have a small piece of land of their own, and cultivate it along with others' land as sharecroppers or subsistence farmers. Others are processors and small traders, mostly dealing in crop processing and trading. Even the latter have to mix agricultural toil with business. These are the families where the whole family: father, mother and children has to be involved in the work. The mother is usually extremely busy on two fronts,the family chores and the crop processing. Naturally, she depends heavily on the adolescent daughters on both counts and cannot afford to be without their assistance for long. Similarly, the father depends on the adolescent boys, sometimes even before they have reached adolescence.

While the families do not actually starve, the nutrition level is low. There is not much cash income. As a result, other household needs, e.g. housing and clothes, are often neglected. Even though primary education is free, and textbooks are supplied, the costs of exercise books, stationery, occasional fees such as examination fees, tend to be burdensome.

Parents themselves are mostly illiterate and cannot help their children with education, nor can they pursue the issues of education against these odds. Their outlook to gender is traditionally discriminatory in relation to the girl child, who is regarded more as a burden than an asset. There is, therefore, not much incentive for girls' education, especially after they reach puberty.

Young people from these families are often school dropouts and are engaged in various economic activities, some contributing a marginal and others a significant income for the family. The CMES education programme targets these young people and tries to encourage them into the field of education. Once they enrol in a CMES school they have to devote a lot of time to the school programme, and cannot really continue to pursue in full what they were doing before. The immediate loss of income and convenience to the family may be substantial, and even critical. Naturally, it is not easy to persuade young people and their families in such a situation, and CMES had to evolve appropriate strategies to achieve this difficult task.

The age range for the out-of-school youth targeted by CMES is quite wide. It is between 11 and 20 for the regular students while older students may be involved in the graduate work, continuing education and adolescent girls' programme supporting the education programme.

Programme and Strategies: Mode, Scope, Quality

The Organisation of the System

The CMES programme to address the educational needs of out-of-school youth is its Basic School System (BSS), which has evolved since 1981. The system consists of three kinds of schools:

i)   Basic Schools (BS);

ii) Advanced Basic Schools (ABS); and

iii) Rural Technology Centre (RTC).

In one area of some 20 villages, 16 BS, 4 ABS and one RTC are typically clustered into a unified BSS unit to offer a series of educational opportunities.

The BS takes care of early primary level education in a two-year programme, providing a foundation in literacy, numeracy, and basic knowledge in approaches to the physical and social environment. The ABS completes primary and lower secondary education (up to a approximately Grade VIII) in a compact three-year course. The RTC does the same, but offers wider opportunities and graduate work, and also acts as the resource centre for the whole unit. All these schools provide technical education along with general education.

The General Strategy

The BSS offers general education, skills training, practice in business skills at market level, income-generation and other life-skills, offering immediate improvement in the quality of life. All of this is achieved within a unique curriculum where the activities are fully integrated into a general education, its three components being:

i) general education;

ii) technology skills training and practice in income-generation; and

iii) "home-to-home work" in health and environment.

This strategy overcomes the problems encountered by the target group in remaining in education. The BSS integrated approach addresses the issues of opportunity: cost, relevance and quality-education, all within the same package.

Opportunity cost: Cash income-generation is part of the school programme, starting from enrolment. The potential steadily increases as skills training and practice progresses. Students can also practise trades learned at school outside school hours using the campus facilities.

Relevance: Out-of-school youth find this system specifically organised for them, and that it is sensitive to their needs. Although they are offered a wholesome curriculum, this is not meant to be simply a preparation for the next stage. Rather, each stage here is complete in itself and results in immediate, practical empowerment and capacity-building. The "home-to-home work" allows them to translate their education into improvement in quality of life, both at home and within the neighbourhood. Families as well as students, can see education at work.

Quality education: Much of the participatory, analytical and problem-solving methods so valued in quality education, can be introduced in a natural way through practical interaction within the various components. Students can draw on problems from their own life as well as practical activities and deal with these within the framework of literacy, mathematics and essential knowledge-based general education. On the other hand, they can apply these abilities to practical and income-generating work, making them richer and more satisfied. The school day is divided into inner-campus and outer-campus times. The former offers tuition, while the latter offers opportunities for skills training, practice, "home-to-home" work, etc. This crossover can enrich their lives. Many of the educational aids come from real life practices too. Apart from these special ingredients, the normal elements of quality education are catered for through relevant teacher training, classroom practice and teaching methods. The fact that the students are mature, motivated young people earning their own living, is fully exploited. The textbooks and supplementary material developed by CMES reflect this. BSS has developed a methodology for quality education for its own specific needs entitled Fifteen Methods.

Supportive Programmes for Empowerment and Continuity

To strengthen the Basic School System for out-of-school youth, and to ensure retention and post-school continuity for both adolescent boys and girls, CMES has undertaken several, important, supportive programmes. They are as follows:

Adolescent Girls' Programme (AGP)

The BSS experience shows that girls in traditional society have been doubly disadvantaged because of gender discrimination. They are less likely to continue in school after puberty, and less likely to be enrolled in second chance education, especially if that second chance means a substantial education package, demanding involvement and continuity. They are subjected to a loss of rights both within and outside the family, as well as child marriage, restrictions and neglect. This robs them of their natural exuberant adolescence and does away with all hopes of further education and development. CMES started an Adolescent Girls'

Programme (AGP) in 1991 to try to empower girls against these odds. Over the years, this has become a very successful and recognised CMES programme, giving rise to similar efforts at home and abroad.

With BSS units as its base and vehicle, AGP organises girls into local "associations" of approximately 20 girls, and "solidarity units" of approximately 400 girls. Led by AGP teachers and pioneer girls, the "associations" hold weekly gender sessions and the "solidarity units" arrange monthly conventions. Continued education: skills training, awareness and practice in relation to general health, reproductive health, rights, freedom of movement, independence etc are combined with other issues such as personality and leadership, equal opportunities, freedom from discrimination and child marriage within the AGP practical package.

Two important aspects of the programme within continuing education relate to the above issues and the adoption of non-stereotypical attitudes to making a living. Parents are closely involved in the programme which improves motivation. The empowerment process gradually becomes more effective and widespread. Boys have been included in the programme, and a special programme for young couples maintains the continuity beyond marriage.

Graduate Work

Continued income-generating work for recent graduates has been organised within BSS. This serves several purposes. The graduates have a breathing space where they can try to start their own business or look for appropriate employment. They do not feel helpless once out of the system. Many of the graduates in this kind of work take leadership roles as they have better skills and experience compared with the existing students. To assist in their continuing education some the graduates have been given the positions of Teaching Assistants in both inner-campus and outer-campus classes. While this enhances staffing levels, it also enables the schools to accept bigger job orders and to start bigger income-generating projects.

Continuing Education

At every Advanced Basic School, there is a Continuing Education Programme, late in the afternoon after normal school hours. This is a facility for BSS graduates to practise and develop their educational competencies. They organise themselves into study circles, use the library created for them and take up group activities. A teacher facilitates, but most of the programme is peer-organised. They are also encouraged to contribute to the cost of upkeep from their own income.

The Policy on Curriculum and Materials

The BSS curriculum reflects the basic education plan for out-of-school youth. It covers a syllabus roughly the equivalent of Grade I to Grade VIII, while including the curriculum for the other two components – technical skills and "home-to-home" work.

The General Education Curriculum

A compatibility with the National Curriculum is attempted for several reasons:

(i) After graduating from BSS some students may still be old enough, and may have developed the motivation to join the formal stream at an appropriate level.

ii) For certain kinds of employment an equivalence of a certain level of formal education is demanded. BSS wants to establish such equivalence with the formal sector.

iii) BSS students should not feel that their education is an inferior one. On the other hand, nothing essential for practical purposes is left out, rather much more is added in terms of the competencies and skills acquired.

In spite of the general compatibility, however, there is a lot of scope for a briefer, more compact curriculum through logical reorganisation, and that is what has been done in the BSS curriculum.

In this reorganised form, the lower grades include literacy (Bangla), arithmetic, and a combined subject of essential knowledge entitled Country, Environment and Technology. The higher grades gradually add English, geometry and algebra, basic science, and basic social sciences (including history, geography and some elements of civics and economics). In the reorganisation, the emphasis is more on understanding, practice, application and adoption than on information which is only relevant to rote learning.

As for basic literacy and numeracy, the policy is to put into practice whatever is learned right from the first day, without waiting for an improved vocabulary or even for a complete grasp of the whole alphabet. Practical exercises, including the suggested real life activities, form the focus of each section of the curriculum.

The Technical Education Curriculum

The technical part of education is divided into technologies for short term training and those for extended training. The former are simply learned within months, but are practised and applied in the longer term. These include candle-making, writing, chalk-making, ballpoint pen-making, soap-making, raising nursery saplings, etc. Most of these can be taught even at the Basic School level by the trained generalist teacher, and have very simple books of instruction.

The longer term training skills have a structured curriculum intended to be dispensed over two to three years, leading to gradual expertise. So far, they include carpentry, garment-making, fabric design – tie-dye, batik, block printing, etc., – grafting and budding in plants, masonry, poultry, sericulture, welding, biofertilising, mushroom cultivation, metalcraft, food processing, engine maintenance, pottery, the technique of the electrician, computer operation, etc. While the emphasis is on the practical skills of the trade, the theoretical basis is not neglected. A simplified theoretical background, along with essential calculations and drawings for each area, is included within the curriculum. To facilitate the teaching of these skills, drawing and mapping are regularly practised within the general education course of BSS.

The Home-to-Home Work Curriculum

This basically concentrates on health and environmental intervention at the local level. The curriculum includes the basic science and technology behind such work and the techniques to needed for implementation. The content includes:

i)   improved stoves, saving biomass and preventing smoke;

ii)   toilets and other basic sanitation;

iii)   composting out of waste biomass;

iv)   vermicomposting;

v) immunisation programmes;

vi) First Aid in common maladies, e.g. the making and use of oral rehydration solution for diarrhoea.

vii) tree plantation;

viii) measurement of nutritional status;

ix) simple repairs ; and

x) disaster preparation.

Materials and Aids

The approach of BSS towards educating out-of-school youth is well-researched and thoroughly innovative. Naturally, this requires appropriate material to deliver. CMES developed much of this within its curriculum. All the characteristics of BSS are reflected within the textbooks and supplementary books published by CMES specifically for this purpose. Books published by others including the formal sector are also used when found appropriate.

The supplementary material developed by CMES included: a series of nine books entitled Environment Science Series; a series of four books entitled Rural Technology Series; an inspiring book to develop gender awareness; a book on songs, cultural development and physical fitness; and a series of charts entitled Education and Workcharts. A monthly magazine has been published with interesting content for adolescent students, providing them with a variety of fresh reading material.

It has already been mentioned that the technical and environmental activities of BSS students provide a veritable laboratory for general studies in science and environment. But over and above these materials, teachers have been trained to organise their own aids for demonstration of scientific phenomena and for the 'do-it-yourself' type of learning. For this purpose, BSS has developed a low-cost, basic, portable, science experimentation kit with simple, easily available materials, enclosed within a small, metal case. Every school has one of these, and students can perform experiments of their own with the help of an illustrated guidebook.

The Strategy for Mainstreaming

Mainstreaming in the case of BSS mainly means mainstreaming into the world of educated work and further development, rather than into formal education. BSS is, therefore, designed to relate to this strategy of mainstreaming. Educational competencies and technical skills which would be demanded in the world of work emphasised, tested and duly certified.

Certification mentions the detailed competencies, so that the potential employer or the institution of further education or training will understand the level of competency and skills attained. However, as has already been mentioned, some students can join the formal education system at an appropriate level, and there is adequate compatibility and certification if they wish to do so. Out-of-school adolescents can therefore come back to mainstream formal education at any stage.

New possibilities have recently opened up so that BSS graduates can join Vocational Training Institutes (VTIs) in the formal sector and work their way towards an alternative stream of formal education leading to a Technology Secondary School Certificate (SSC). It is hoped that in future more BSS graduates will take advantage of this opportunity to pursue further education.

Income-Generation

It is student income-generation, immediate and potential, that has made the BSS so appropriate for out-of-school youth. The opportunity for income-generation occurs because the products and services created through the practice of technology are actually marketed. Here education takes place against the backdrop of real life and at the market level. A revolving initial fund can thus give students the opportunity to practise again and again while, at the same time, keeping remunerating them with cash. At the same time, the students can be aware of the potential of a career with even better skills and income prospects, within a few years. These few years in school provide them with a direct experience of real life business too.

To make this strategy work, the skills training and practice have to be at a business level. There are built-in mechanisms within the teacher/student teams for the production, management, quality control and of course marketing. Most of the marketing takes place at the local level. Practical skills, therefore, have to be closely related to local demand. *here! here!*

Some of the products are marketed in towns and cities, and the Rural Technology Centre in every unit takes responsibility for the development and implementation of such marketing. Marketing involves promotion and a great deal of interaction with the community. This is a very important characteristic of the BSS. Out-of-school youth who are enrolled in BSS are ideally suited for such interaction. In fact, their education demands and benefits from this kind of close interaction.

Educational Testing

Educational testing in BSS is continuous as well as periodic. Class and school tests *one* are at the school level. The unit organises a monthly test, while there are two central tests conducted in all the units.

The tests are of two types. One is the standard test, following more or less similar methods to those used in formal schools. The other is the competency test. For the latter, test batteries have been devised to measure reading, writing, comprehension, verbal and written expression, mathematical ability and knowledge base. These can indicate which level a student is at, irrespective of his/her class. Each student can helped individually, according to his/her test results.

Teachers and Teacher Training

Each Basic School has one teacher, who is usually a young woman with a local, secondary school certificate. The ABS has two teachers and an assistant teacher. The former have higher secondary certificates, and the latter a secondary certificate.

The RTC has four senior teachers, usually diploma holders in technical education. One of the senior teachers is also in charge of the unit. The senior teachers have, over and above the usual teaching responsibilities for a RTC, the responsibility for visiting BS and ABS in the unit as guest teachers.

The RTC has five assistant teachers who are technicians with some schooling and proficiency in one or more trades included within the curriculum. They conduct the technical courses and lead the income-generation programme.

The teachers are all meticulously trained in BSS methods and in the technical skills included within the system. There are usually 7-15 days of initial training at recruitment. From then on there are bi-monthly, short refreshers. Special training is organised for such subjects as specific technology, monitoring, gender, "home-to-home work", marketing, etc. All training is of the hands-on variety, conducted in a participatory manner with all the modern training techniques. The CMES Training Department organises such training in its Field Training Centres as well as at the Central Training Centre. BSS, being an integrated education package consisting of several components, teacher motivation and teacher training, is vital for its success.

Monitoring and Management

The BS and ABS are monitored regularly by senior teachers from the RTC of the unit, when they visit the schools (approximately once a week) as guest teachers. Less frequently (once a month), monitors from the Central Monitoring Department of BSS at the "Service Centre" in Dhaka visit various units to monitor performance. All the aspects of BSS come into the monitoring process. Apart from the factors affecting quality education and skills attainment, the interface between general education and skills practice for livelihood is given particular attention.

The individual findings in monitoring are used for immediate intervention for improvement. At the same time, the commonalties which emerge from such monitoring are analysed and reviewed for necessary policy guidance. Effective monitoring tools have been developed so that quick assessments can be made. This is important for a system which involves many different aspects.

The unit organiser (UO) or the headteacher in each unit is in charge of that unit. The UO is supported by the team of senior teachers in the management task, each of whom has a specific management responsibility. As they themselves are also the teachers in the RTC and guest teachers (monitors) in BS and ABS, management is integrated within the actual day-to-day operation of the system. The unit management can make necessary policy decisions within the general guideline of the BSS.

The central management of BSS is the responsibility of the CMES Service Centre in Dhaka. To provide management and support services to BSS, the Service

Centre is departmentalised, with various specialised tasks on the one hand, and on the other, task forces mustering expertise from various departments. Thus, the department as well as an extra-departmental task force may address tasks such as research, training, materials development, monitoring, dissemination, etc. There is a Co-ordination Secretariat to co-ordinate the whole management system.

The Evaluation and Criteria of Success

The Basic School System has been in operation for about 20 years now. It has been evaluated internally and externally during this period. There is a Research and Development Department within the CMES Service Centre which organises periodic studies on the effectiveness of various strategies adopted by BSS.

The following are some of the aspects being evaluated:

i)   achievements in education through testing the competencies attained;

ii)   the effectiveness of education in terms of its immediate application;

iii)   achievements in skills training;

iv)   the capacity for marketable production;

v)   the employability of graduates; their retention of education skills and income-generation capabilities;

vi)   the level of gender empowerment;

vii) the utilisation of research and development efforts within BSS; and

viii the effectiveness of dissemination and replication efforts.

For management and evaluation purposes, the following indicators of achievement are used:

i)   the enrolment and completion rate in BSS;

ii)   the success level in education competencies and technical skills;

iii)   employment and self-employment after completion;

iv) income-generation for students and for CMES;

v) community support for BSS;

vi)enrolment and retention in Continuing Education Programme;

vii) the level of participation in Adolescent Girls' Programme; and

viii)the number of significant livelihood achievements and social consequences.

The Policy Adopted to Limit Costs

CMES has undertaken an ambitious programme within NFE for out-of-school youth, in the sense that it not only addresses literacy-based education needs, but it also addresses the young people's livelihood issues through a technology-based approach. But in spite of this, it can keep the system low-cost and replicable. The unit cost per pupil is of the same order as primary and early secondary education in the formal sector, in spite of the fact that everything is supplied and education includes technical education. The key lies in the CMES approach to the whole issue; the school and the programme should match seamlessly with the rural life and surroundings of the local people. The schoolhouse, campus, facilities, and general atmosphere all organised very simply, not unlike the local homesteads and work places, and of course there is nothing alienating or intimidating even for the humblest of families.

CMES has demonstrated that the quality of education and the effectiveness of the programme do not have much to do with the sophistication of the surroundings and facilities, but more to do with the sincerity of those carrying out the programme. Simplicity is therefore a boon. As for the personnel involved in the programme, young men and women of modest backgrounds but with a great deal of enthusiasm have been entrusted with various aspects of the programme, rather than choosing highly qualified experts. It has been demonstrated that the former can implement innovations just as well as the latter, and may also value the spirit of the enterprise more than the form. The important requirement is sustained in-house training in CMES methods.

This policy approach has not only helped to keep costs down, but has also made the whole programme more effective from the point of view of out-of-school youth from disadvantaged families. Emphasis has been placed on peer-organised leadership, so that many of the graduates could develop a new personal skills within the programme, and have joined later as assistants and teachers.

The following factors also helped to keep costs low:

i) The land and schoolhouse for the BS come from the beneficiary families and the land for ABS and RTC come from local donors.

ii) At the BS level, the parents take care of the upkeep of the school, and safeguard its facilities.

iii) Most of the furniture, equipment, educational aids and even writing implements such as chalk, and ball-point pens are produced within the system, as part of technology training and practice.

iv) Students make a voluntary contribution to school funds out of their own income: this is small but gives them a sense of involvement;

v) Rooms, space and facilities have multiple uses wherever possible;

vi) Part of the profits created by sales of the products goes towards operating the school and contributes to finances;

vii) The technologicsl expertise of the teachers and senior students, as well as the equipment and facilities available for technology training, are put to further use in short courses organised for the general public – mostly young people beyond the targeted group. These are fee-paying courses, and generate some income for the system. Similarly, training is offered to other organisations for a fee. Many of these strategies are gradually becoming more effective and are expected to contribute further to the cost reduction and sustainability of the programme.

Interaction with the Community

BSS works very closely with the community, in particular with the target group community. The second chance education offered by BSS for out-of-school youth would work well if the families themselves responded to the innovative approaches of the project and contributed in their various ways. This is why community participation is emphasised in the following ways:

i)   The comparatively well-to-do members of the community donate land for ABS and RTC. They do this as a philanthropic gesture to the cause.

ii) Beneficiary families provide the use of an outhouse in their homestead as a BS schoolhouse, with the surrounding areas for outer-campus use.

iii) The parents meet once a month to review school management, programme, attendance, and achievements.

iv) Open days for the parents, community members and potential students are observed to help them understand the scope of this system. The annual student/teacher/parent day is a festive occasion.

v)   The community is the immediate patron of the products and services offered by BSS. In fact, success depends on the community purchasing these products and services.

vi) In the Home-to-Home Programme within BSS, students and teachers work alongside the neighbourhood families in their homesteads regularly every week, developing a working bond between the school and the community.

vii) The community supports the BSS by enrolling in its fee-paying short courses.

Available Resources and Support

Community support has already been mentioned. CMES started the BSS with this community support and whatever it could muster in terms of its own resources. Then, with the need for the system to attain a certain size, international donors came forward to become partners with CMES, providing the bulk of the developmental and operational costs.

Over the years, cost sharing on behalf of the BSS has gradually increased. But even so, it is still highly dependent on donor funding. The strategy for self-sustainability has to work much more effectively to change this situation. But hope lies within the interest that the mainstream is now showing towards CMES intervention in the education of out-of-school youth. If this interest materialises into the adoption of the model, then it is to be hoped that national government, local government and the corporate sector may take up the major responsibility of funding the system; the community and the system itself would do the rest.

Collaboration and Partnerships

CME has been working closely with its development partners on BSS. Its dissemination efforts through the production of a series of materials (both print and audiovisual), seminars and workshops, and local collaboration with other organisations, has resulted in an understanding of the system, and a demand for partnership and collaboration.

CMES has strong links with relevant policymakers: government (including PMED, DNFE), NGOs, donors, UN bodies, development banks, etc. for this mode of education for out-of-school youth. There has been a positive response from each sector.

CMES has helped others, including UN bodies, to formulate their own programme in the light of its BSS and AGP. Various NGOs have come forward for the replication of the model. CMES materials, and training has been requested by other organisations, including those of government. This process of extension through partnership has much greater scope and will be properly addressed now.

Success Achieved so Far

CMES started BSS as an experimental project in 1981. Over the years it has extended itself to 17 units in 17 different areas of Bangladesh. At any given time it has been served about 20,000 students, mostly out-of-school youth. More than 50 per cent of the students are female. It has produced more than 100,000 graduates during these years. Many of them have had enough motivation to join mainstream formal education. But most have chosen a skilled career (with many of them electing continuing education).

The Adolescent Girls' Programme, supportive to BSS, has had its own remarkable success. It has a present membership of some 6,000 girls. Their empowerment through the programme is creating a significant impact on local society as far as gender and development issues are concerned. Many of the girls have gained technical skills through the programme and have adopted non-stereotypical livelihood activities. A total of TK20,475,900 (about US$372,290) has been disbursed within the AGP micro- credit scheme. The programme has been adopted as a model for more significant interventions by others including UNICEF and UNDP.

In spite of its unorthodox school system, BSS could convince all concerned, including the NFE mainstream and the government agencies, of its effectiveness and inevitability. BSS was invited to join the government General Education Project (GEP), and participated in the project over three years, working closely with government and keeping all the characteristics of BSS intact. CMES has played a major role within CAMPE (Campaign for Popular Education), the apex organisation for the education NGOs of Bangladesh, and is currently acting as a member of its executive body. There has been increasing interest in the CMES model of education for out-of-school youth, and the sustained demonstration by BSS of its feasibility and effectiveness, even within such a substantial operation has been brought home to many, including DNFE and PMED.

The Prospects of Replication and Sustainability

BSS is in the process of replication, and it is therefore actively disseminated among potential replicators and stakeholders: community members, government policy implementers, NGOs, UN agencies, donors and civil organisations. Already, the system has been acceptable to some replicators who have the potential to make it an effective means of education for out-of-school youth over a wide area. In the past, various organisations have adopted the model for their specific needs. CODES Bangladesh, an NGO working in urban areas, implemented it for young in an urban slum, most of whom were ex-garment workers, unemployed and uneducated. Somaj Dorpon, an NGO working in a northern district of the country, adopted it for its rural programme. Grameen Shikhya, a subsidiary of Grameen Bank, has adopted the model for the education of young people who are working in a predominantly weaving area. With an organisation such as Grameen Shikhya adopting it, the model has a very good prospect of being widely replicated.

PLAN-International, an international NGO working actively in the field of education in various areas of Bangladesh, has decided that in the CMES model it has found an effective means of reaching out-of-school youth. A method of implementing this model in the PLAN areas of work is now being worked out.

ASROI, an NGO working with the indigenous, ethnic people in the western districts of the country, has asked CMES to help in the implementation of the model for this target group. The details are now being considered.

The potential replicators are particularly attracted by the element of sustainability in the model: through the participation of the community, the close integration with livelihood, the potential for income-generation for the operation of the system, and the impact on the economic life of the community, including improved quality of life and the donors' increased willingness to provide financial support. All of these factors create an optimistic prospect for the ultimate adoption of this model as a viable NFE effort, targeting this very important target group – out-of-school youth.

The UCEP Programme

The Target Group

The Underprivileged Children's Educational Programme (UCEP) started as an international NGO in 1972 to create educational opportunities for child workers in urban areas. The programme has been working in the major cities of Bangladesh with the same aim and the same target group.

Surveys showed that many of the underprivileged children of the urban areas in Bangladesh are either engaged in various small workshops or factories, or less formally as domestic servants, construction workers, porters, cigarette vendors, shoeshine boys, etc. Their life and work is strenuous and often dangerous. But poverty forces them into this kind of employment, away from education which is their natural right.

The UCEP programme targeted these children and young people in such a way that to begin with, they are not taken away from their present work, but are offered a combination of conventional education and skills training, which will lead them away from this drudgery towards a higher quality of life.

A study of recent UCEP students showed that most of the students' families have migrated from the rural areas for various reasons – 42.68 per cent because of economic hardship, 36.83 per cent in search of work, 6.93 per cent because of river erosion, and 6.89 per cent because of loss of land. The most common family size 5-6 family members (46.82 per cent). Most of them have a daily family income of between US$ 1 to US$ 1.4 They live in overcrowded city slums.

The age of the students is 10 to 12 years (42.68 per cent), 12 to 14 (39.95 per cent) and 14 to 16 (14.21 per cent). The major occupations of the students include domestic servants (13.55 per cent), factory workers (11.03 per cent), day labourers (5.90 per cent), shop assistants (8.12 per cent), small traders and vendors (19.31 per cent), workshop workers (5.18 per cent), tiffin carriers (4.17 per cent), tailors (3.62 per cent), rickshaw/pushcart pullers (3.55 per cent), hotel/mess boys (2.91 per cent), garbage collectors (2.24 per cent), and porters (1.22 per cent). Their cash income is meagre, though many of them get food while at work.

Programme and Strategies: Mode, Scope, Quality

The General Organisation of Education

The UCEP programme organises NFE schools for the general education of 11+ boys and 10+ girls in the cities away from the target group of children. This lasts four-and-a-half years and covers Grade I to Grade VIII. From the graduates of these schools, UCEP selects some of them for its technical schools, where they attend trade courses lasting from six months to two years. These accommodate some 1,350 students. For those students who cannot gain a place in the technical schools, or for those who have to stop general education at Grade V, there are arrangements for para-trade training centres which offer short term training in various simpler trades. Set up only recently, the para-trade centres train only a small number of students – 192 in total.

Strategies for Education

UCEP General Education Schools

- **Proximity:** UCEP has built its own schoolhouses in the areas of the cities where there is a concentration of slum-dwelling children and young people. The adolescent target group can easily access these nearby schools without affecting their work and income.

- **Flexible time:** The nature of their work makes a certain time of the day suitable for school attendance for the target group. This varies from occupation to occupation. Taking this into consideration, UCEP schools are run according to three shifts, each lasting two-and-a-half hours. Working children, therefore, can choose any of these shifts as their convenient school time for school.

- **Compact course:** UCEP has organised the curriculum and school days in such a way that the usual one year course for the formal school takes only six months here. Thus eight classes can be completed within only four-and-a-half years.

- **Improved ratio:** The teacher-student ratio here is 1:30, which is ideal in order to take adequate care of each individual student.

- **All materials supplied:** UCEP bears all the costs for education, including those of textbooks, exercise books, stationery, etc.

UCEP Technical Schools

- Technical school students are selected from among the graduates of the general schools on the basis of competence. The main aim of these technical schools is to create skilled technicians from the working boys and girls, so that they in turn can bring about a change in the socio-economic situation of their families.

- The selection of trade and curriculum are formulated with an eye to employment opportunities. Changes to formulation are brought about in accordance with evaluation of the demands from employers and industries.

- Training is learner-centred, emphasis being given to trainee participation. Close contact is kept with potential employers, so that a collaborative programme can be maintained.

- During training students are exposed to the real life environment and to the rules followed in the factory. This prepares them for employment and the proper discharge of their responsibilities within this kind of employment.

- The areas of training are as follows: automobile repairs; welding and general fitting; electrical; refrigeration and air-conditioning; electronics; printing; carpentry; garments; wool knitting; garment finishing; textile spinning; textile weaving; and textile knitting.

UCEP Para-trade Training Centres

Here a number of UCEP students are trained in some appropriate skills in accordance with the demands of the labour market. These are: electrical decoration and housewiring; embroidery and fabric decoration with metal foilwork; sign board and banner writing; screen-printing; wood-carving; motor mechanics; leathercraft and tailoring.

Training is arranged in two shifts in each of these trades, each shift including 12 trainees. Two such para-trade centres in Dhaka and Chittagong take a total of 192 students. The para-trades are open to anyone who has completed up to any grade between the fifth and the eighth grade. Training in the trade takes six months. In one of the para-trade centres, some disabled children are attending trade courses along with the other students.

UCEP Employment Programme

UCEP feels that it is not enough to provide out-of-school working children with general and technical education without trying to help them get employment in the relevant sector. There would then remain the risk of these skills not being used, resulting in the continuation of poverty. Therefore, one of the components of the UCEP programme is designed to ensure employment for its graduates.

The strategy for ensuring such employment is to keep close contact with potential employers – factories, industries, government and private organisations and others. In fact, much of the education programme is designed with employers' opinions in mind. The following activities facilitate this employment programme:

i) To prepare a job seeker's list: An up-to-date list is maintained of graduates of general schools, technical schools and para-trade centres who need jobs. The list would contain a CV and a competency description for each job seeker.

ii) Job market survey: This survey leads to a database on all potential employers and their possible demand for skilled workers.

iii) Job hunting weeks: These are intensive efforts lasting for two weeks, several times a year, when the job placement officer/trainer visits various employment places along with graduates. They try to convince employers of the abilities of the job seekers.

iv) Employers' days: These special days are observed from time to time. Employers are invited on the day to visit the UCEP programmes and to talk with the staff and graduates.

The Policy on Curriculum and Materials

General Education

The National Curriculum is used with a few modifications to suit working children's needs. All the marginal competencies (53 in total) of the National Curriculum are maintained, but the syllabus has been condensed.

Classes I to V are regarded as preparatory level. Subjects that are included at this level are Bangla, English, Maths, Religion and Fine Arts. Classes VI to VIII comprise the lower secondary level. This level includes Bangla, English, Maths, General Science, Social Science and Religion. These subjects take up four periods during each shift of two-and-a-half hours.

UCEP uses national textbooks, as well as some of its own supplementary books. The latter include those on environment, family, health and child rights. These reading materials are prepared with the socio-economic background of the students in mind. Other materials used include cards, visual aids, charts, and display boards.

The various elements of student-centred education, such as group discussion, role-play, question and answer, assigned job, narration of experience, project work, etc., are used in the classroom.

Technical Education

The technical courses in the technical schools and para-trade centres are organised in response to job market demands. The curriculum and competencies are mainly dictated by this factor. Changes implemented from time to time also occur because of this. The other factor which influences the curriculum of technical schools is the attempt to keep a general competency with the National Curriculum in vocational education. This not only widens employability, but also facilitates the continuation of vocational training in higher institutions for those who decide to continue. All graduates of the technical schools have to complete a six-month on-the-job training placement in a factory or relevant workplace, as a part of the system.

The Strategy for Mainstreaming

The UCEP general education programme is compatible with the primary and lower secondary levels of the formal stream. So graduates of the UCEP general schools can be mainstreamed into formal schools in cases where students can do without a full-time, earning, occupation.

More possibilities, however, open up in cases where general school graduates go on to the UCEP technical schools, graduate from there, and then get mainstreamed into the government vocational training schools.

The UCEP Vocational Training Programme has been accredited by the Bangladesh Technical Education Board, which allows graduates to take examinations conducted by the Board. So this UCEP programme is linked to the structure of vocational training in the national stream. Through this path, formal vocational training facilities would be really accessible to working children from urban slums who have a genuine motivation to become skilled workers and practise a trade .

Income-Generation

UCEP has demonstrated that working for a salary and also attending school can go together. It has organised its education programme in such a way that working youth can continue their work while attending a suitable shift at school. Th income, however, has to be earned out of school rather than within school. Therefore, although they are constantly improving themselves through education, their work environment does not change significantly until they graduate and change jobs.

The UCEP school system creates new potential for income-generation with the help of its employment programme. This is most effective for graduates of the technical schools – about 95 per cent of them are assured of income-generating employment. But only a few enrolled students can progress to the technical schools. For the rest, jobs are not so assured. The UCEP employment programme has been successful in putting 60 per cent of these graduates into work. General education and technical education are separated in the UCEP system: the latter follows the former for a selected number of students who can be accommodated in the technical schools. The introduction of para-trade centres has potentially improved the situation by encouraging an increased number of graduates and dropouts into a more modest form of technical education. This promises to have a better impact on the employment rates of non-technical school graduates.

Educational Testing

The following measures in educational testing have ensured improved learning achievement among UCEP students:

i)   the setting of question papers for examinations on the basis of marginal competencies;

ii) question papers set by schools in one division are moderated by those in another division;

iii) teachers and supervisors from one school conduct tests in another;

iv) similarly, the papers are examined by teachers from another school;

v)   the two terminal examinations at the end of the two levels, i.e. for Class V and Class VIII, are centrally organised; and

vii) a monthly examination system has been introduced.

Teachers and Teacher Training

UCEP schools have qualified teachers trained in this particular method of NFE. Technical schools and para-trade centres have expert instructors. In all, there are about 800 education workers in the programme. To train them and to develop their skills, UCEP has a separate unit called the Human Resources Development Component.

Teachers are given in-house training that includes basic training for teachers, as well as subject training. Apart from training in school subjects and methodology, some subjects, which are particularly important for the UCEP target group such as child rights, are also included. The following is a list of some of the specific training areas offered:

• social work;

• teaching process;

- child psychology;

- budget and control;

- computers;

- subject specific methods of teaching;

- methods of development for weak students;

- school management;

- oral training for teachers and instructors;

- child rights;

- educational aids; and

- the development of entrepreneurs.

The Training Cell studies the training needs in each case and then prepares the training modules in a participatory manner. There is a special need within UCEP to train the instructors involved in the technical skills training. The most significant part of this takes place in the technical training institutions and the industries where the instructors are regularly sent for training.

UCEP education management personnel are also trained in appropriate institutions, both at home and abroad. Many of them have received training in countries such as the UK, Denmark, Thailand, India, Nepal and the Philippines. The Human Resources Development Component of UCEP also trains personnel from other organisations within and outside the country.

Monitoring and Management

Teachers in UCEP schools are responsible for more than just teaching. They monitor student attendance, and students' wellbeing in school and at home. If a student remains absent from school for three consecutive days, the teacher visits his/her home or workplace, talks to the parents, guardians or bosses, tries to find out the reasons and effect a solution.

The UCEP project is divided into several divisions, and each division is administered by a divisional co-ordinator and his/her staff. Teachers send monthly attendance and dropout statements to their divisional co-ordinator, which are then forwarded to UCEP headquarters. The data is regularly reviewed for the necessary action.

Teachers keep in-close contact with the families and employers of the working children, and interact with them personally and in community meetings organised by the teachers. The management of the school system is also closely related to this process, and has resulted in an improved attendance rate of 92 per cent in 1997-98, as against 50-60 per cent in the earlier years. The dropout rate has come down to 51 per cent, from about 15-90 per cent.

Interaction with the Community

Interaction takes place in the following ways:

i)   the curriculum and the selection of trades are influenced by the opinions and demands of the community;

ii) assistance is received from the community while establishing a school;

iii) regular meetings are held with community members in the school;

iv) parents, guardians and employers are regularly contacted by teachers about attendance;

v)   potential employers are always kept informed, and their opinions are given importance in policy formulation.

Cost and Replication

A philanthropic New Zealander, L A. Cheyne, established UCEP in 1972, organising financial grants from international donors. Right from the start, no cost was spared to make the education provided a quality one – investing in schoolhouses, facilities, personnel, teacher training, monitoring and management.

The equipment and facilities for technical education are of a high standard and therefore capital-intensive. This form of education can, however, take only a limited number of students at a time. As a result, the unit cost of technical education has been particularly high, almost six times as high as that for general education. UCEP general education also has a unit cost higher than that of many NGO-NFE projects, but is still of the same order as formal primary and lower secondary schools.

As UCEP depends on a high level of cost being covered through donor support (96 per cent of the cost), the education programme has a rather limited capacity for replication as far as economic outlay is concerned. However, its effectiveness is amply demonstrated for urban, out-of-school young people, and strategies can be worked out to make the model more cost-effective while keeping the essentials intact.

Success Achieved So Far

Ten UCEP general schools have been established in different parts of Dhaka city, with a total intake of 3,086 students. More schools were added in other cities of the country – Chittagong, eight, Khulna, six and Rajshahi, two. Now 20,323 students are receiving their education in these schools, 30 in total.

There are three technical (vocational) schools, one in each of the cities of Dhaka, Chittagong and Khulna. More recently, para-trade centres have been set up in Dhaka and Chittagong. The total number of students in technical schools is 1,350 and in para-trade centres, 192.

Approximately 50 per cent of UCEP graduates from its general schools could be given some sort of vocational training, and almost all those receiving such training were employed in suitable jobs. Of those who could not find places in vocational schools, some 60 per cent could find new and better jobs. A survey shows that in 80 per cent of cases, UCEP students earn TK600 or more per month in their first job, that they have satisfactory employment and that 92 per cent of them think that their socio-economic position has now improved. Whereas 90 per cent of them used to live in the slums, only 10 per cent do so after graduation.

It is not only the students themselves whose fate has been changed through UCEP education. The socio-economic situation of their families has also improved. A recent survey shows that whereas 19 per cent of the students used to support the total living expenses of their family, upon completion of the UCEP programme this has increased to 30 per cent. Similarly, the percentage of those who would bear 25-50 per cent of family expenses has increased from 30 per cent to 70 per cent. UCEP has made young people more capable of supporting their families.

A survey of the employers of UCEP graduates shows that they are satisfied with the loyalty and the discipline of these workers. They can soon overtake the other workers in work expertise because of their education and training. Employer satisfaction has encouraged them to allow their factory shopfloors to be used for on-the-job training of UCEP students.

BRAC Education Programme for Out-of-school Youth

The Target Group

BRAC (formerly Bangladesh Rural Advancement Committee), the biggest NGO in Bangladesh, has a large NFE programme. Its major intervention is NFPE (Non-Formal Primary Education), a three-year programme for 8-10 year olds from disadvantaged families, aiming to facilitate their transfer into mainstream formal education.

BRAC's intervention in the education of out out-of- school youth comes through its programme: Basic Education for Older Children (BEOC), a three-year education course for 11-14 year olds. BRAC's Continued Education Programme, through its library schemes, has also indirectly contributed to the education of adolescents who are no longer at school.

BRAC has tried to address the problems of non-schooling among the older children of poor, rural families, who have to assist their parents in their struggle to make a living. BRAC made its education provision easily accessible to this target group with a specially tailored curriculum and method and by creating books and aids appropriate for situation in life.

Strategies for Education

Innovative Features

- Appropriate life-oriented curriculum and materials for the target group.

- Extensive co-curricular activities to make education useful and enjoyable.

- BEOC has a teacher to student ratio of 1:30.

- Regular supervision to ensure quality.

- 70 per cent of students are female. Almost all teachers are female. _interesting_.

Basic Arrangements in Education

- **Schoolhouse:** One room in which the same group of students are taken from one grade to another till they graduate. The simple schoolhouse belongs to the community, for which normal rent is paid.

- **Teacher:** At least up to 9th grade qualification. A thorough training follows. Each school has one teacher.

- **Curriculum and materials:** The National Curriculum is followed, but this is revised with an eye to making it appropriate, and shortened to suit the target group – out-of-school adolescents. In particular, the curriculum for the higher grades within primary school is condensed. Three years of BEOC is divided into four phases of seven months and one of eight months, each covering a standard grade.

- BRAC develops its own educational materials which are well researched and attentive to the demands of the target group.

In order to add some life skills, supplementary subjects such as health, family and employment are included with the appropriate material.

Monitoring and Management

Parents and local community leaders participate in a School Management Committee. This committee also provides resource teachers, programme organisers, teams in charge, quality managers, regional managers and supervisors to assist teachers, in managing the school. One programme organiser is in charge of 12-15 schools. His/her duty is to supervise twice weekly and to help teachers to correct faults.Resource teachers also supervise schools and conduct parents' meetings.Quality managers play the role of co-ordinators for all personnel involved in supervision and monitoring.

The responsibilities of the School Management Committee are to ensure:

- the regular attendance of learners;

- the regular attendance of teachers; and

- the necessary repairs and maintenance of the schoolhouse.

A monthly parents' meeting is helpful in looking after these issues.

Educational Testing and Evaluation

Daily, weekly and monthly tests are conducted by the teacher. Weak students are given extra help. There is a general assessment after the completion of a three-year course. Written reports are prepared for examination by various levels of management.

Training

The following types of teacher training have been organised:

i) Fifteen-day foundation training: This comprehensive training is organised in a residential training centre. Teachers start the training after a seven-day attachment with a school.

ii) Three-day orientation: This is arranged before the teachers actually start teaching.

iii) One-day refresher: Supervisors organise this on-the-job refresher day once a month, and a review and planning session from month to month.

In addition, there are other special training sessions during school recesses to upgrade teachers' skills. School supervisors also receive such training at various intervals.

Success and Impact

BRAC's BEOC programme has provided a second chance of education for a large number of out-of-school youth, particularly adolescent girls. After graduating from BEOC, many of them pursue further education through the libraries organised by BRAC as a means of continuing education.

There are other profound effects. Child marriage has decreased. New skills are developed, empowering young people. Awareness about health and ecology has increased. Parents are aware of the value of education as well as that of gender equity.

Libraries for Continuing Education

In order to help graduate youth to retain their competencies, BRAC has organised adolescent study circles. A circle starts with about 150 books – mostly on health and the environment. Other books, fiction and non-fiction, as well as magazines and periodicals, are also supplied.

Adolescent girls and young women are especially encouraged to get together and make use of this facility. Some useful livelihood training is taken up in the adolescent study circles, such as on poultry-rearing, nurseries, kitchen gardens, book-binding, etc. The membership of these circles has now increased to more than 6,000. There are also BRAC union libraries which are open to all villagers, as well as BRAC graduates.

Replication

BRAC itself has replicated the model in its thousands of BEOC schools. The model education programme has also been widely replicated by various organisations both at home and abroad. BRAC offers training, reading materials, as well as technical and strategic assistance to the replication efforts.

The DAM Education Programme for Out-of-school Youth

The Target Group

Dhaka Ahsania Mission (DAM), established in 1958 as a social welfare organisation, has in recent years focused its education efforts on facilities called Gonokendra (People's Centres), targeting mainly the new literates and dropout youth as well as adults.

Gonokendra has been organised on the basis that dropout adolescents and newly literate youth and adults who have attended basic literacy courses, and who mostly come from disadvantaged families, cannot usually be accommodated in a formal institution for their further education. One way for their continued education would be through a multi-purpose socialisation education centre accessible to a wide range of people who need it. Gonokendra is such a facility. While it has its specific target group, it is also an education centre for everybody in the locality – men, women, children and adolescents. Most of the beneficiaries are the rural poor of whom 70 per cent are female.

Educational Strategies

General Characteristics

The basic nature of Gonokendra is that of a library, with further facilities for entertainment and social interaction. The possibility of imparting awareness and training in some socially important subjects also exists. Issues of current and local interest can be discussed and debated within Gonokendra.

Gonokendra places emphasis on the role of the community in the establishment, and management and ownership of the facility. A centre serves 75-100 beneficiaries and provides a number of services.

Gonokendra Activities

- **Education:** This comes through the variety of educational material available in Gonokendra. Participants learn through reading by themselves and through subject-centred discussions. A DAM facilitator or a community worker would help them in the process whenever needed.

- **Information:** Useful information for the target group is disseminated through the various current materials from appropriate government or private agencies, held in the Gonokendra centre. These include information about health, technology, finance, the job market, society, environment, culture, etc.

- **Training and work:** Useful initiatives are taken up by Gonokendra participants who are trained by facilitators for such work. The work is also an important learning process, and includes programmes related to gender development, protection of the environment, immunisation, recreation, etc. The work also includes, from time to time, programmes for community development, such as infrastructural ones in transport, afforestation and sanitation.

- **Networking and communication:** Gonokendra facilitates communication and networking among the participants themselves. At the same time, it helps in establishing linkages with the local government, educational institutions, and economic organisations.

Curriculum and Materials

Basic literacy is assumed in the Gonokendra activities. But since most of the participants are newly literate, the emphasis is on easy-to-read materials. An approximate equivalence of Classes 3 and 4 in the National Curriculum is set for most practical purposes.

Once this is assumed, the curriculum for Gonokendra is broad, in accordance with the needs of the participants. The whole exercise is life-oriented, and therefore whatever is demanded from the lives of participants, is included within the curriculum.

The materials available in Gonokendra reflect this wide spectrum of the curriculum. DAM itself produces a rich variety of educational material in its book programme, including booklets, charts, posters, stickers, etc. Similar material from other NGOs and various government departments and agencies is also collected for Gonokendra. Newspapers, newsletters, bulletins, etc. are regularly preserved at the centre. Facilitators and community members themselves are encouraged to create materials of interest. They write local news items, articles, etc., which are put on display in the centre as a mimeo newsletter.

Information and training items on agriculture, poultry and cattle rearing, vegetable production, management of small trades, the organisation of groups, as well as areas such as the environment, sanitation, food, nutrition and health, feature prominently in the curriculum and the materials. Interesting fiction, both for educational purposes and for entertainment, is also not neglected.

Management and Monitoring: Indicators of Success

The basic task of managing and monitoring Gonokendra belongs to the community. There is, therefore, a local management committee consisting of community members. The committee also performs useful functions in the planning and implementation of the programmes of the centre, including training, networking, etc.

The centre is generally open four to five days a week, for two to three hours a day. During this time a facilitator looks after the library and conducts programmes. He/she is also in charge of the collection and creation of the books and materials. DAM fieldworkers and supervisors also conduct various programmes in close collaboration with the local management committee. The fieldworkers act as monitors, sending reports about the centre to DAM headquarters and also maintain communications with government agencies and NGOs.

The DAM Monitoring and Evaluation Unit monitors the programme on the basis of some fixed indicators. These include management aspects, qualitative indicators, quantitative indicators, networking and co-operation, the functions of the supervisors and facilitators, etc. The qualitative indicators cover the content of materials, the creation of materials by the centre, the mobilisation of resources, the impact on income-generation, awareness levels and development activities.

The quantitative indicators include attendance, the number of centres, the number of reading materials, space for the centre, committee meetings, the number of supervision visits, as well as accounting, collection and management of funds.

Staff Training

DAM supervisors and fieldworkers receive training on the various subjects which enable Gonokendra to function. These include gender, environment, socio-cultural activities, etc. Facilitation methods are also covered, such as communication, identification of local resources and their use, community participation, and the development of learner-centred materials.

There is a six-day field level foundation training course, followed by periodic follow-up training. Trainers from the DAM Training Cell conduct this kind of training. There is also training for the members of the local management committee.

Resources, Cost-Effectiveness and Sustainability

Each Gonokendra needs a room, books and materials, furniture and services for facilitation and management. Initially, DAM provides the funds for these needs as well as providing all technical support. The fieldworkers mobilise local funds with the help of the local management committee.

As a centre can serve up to 100 participants and many of the activities are self-motivated and self-organised, the system is cost-effective. The cost per participant is about half of that of a typical NGO NFPE provider.

The sustainability plan for Gonokendra is in place. DAM initiates a centre and funds it for five years. But the centre really belongs to the community, which will have the ultimate responsibility for financing and managing it.

The materials will continue to be collected from community members, government agencies, NGOs, etc. Educated and inspired community members will take over the tasks of facilitation. The first five years of operation will create enough skills among the target group through awareness and income-generation, that they will be able to handle these responsibilities.

Success and Replication

There are 1,072 Gonokendra centres in five districts of the country. The results have been quite successful so far. The basic objective has been to explore feasible and appropriate continuing education for all, with emphasis on newly literate youth. The very fact that they have been motivated to participate in the flexible, self-initiated programmes of the centres shows that this can be a feasible model. The involvement of the community, and the built-in sustainability plan for handing it over to the community, makes it all the more sustainable. The comprehensive impact on the youth of the community has been quite positive so far.

DAM is trying to replicate the Gonokendra model through other partners. It is conducting technical, financial and material collaboration to this end with 20 local organisations. DAM is also collaborating with a large national NGO, ASA, to operate Gonokendra where ASA has microcredit programmes. Similarly, links with a health programme operated by Concern Universal are being considered.

Communities developing for health

A special report for
the Regional Director
of Public Health for
North West England
2000

Edited by Pam Ashton
and Andrew Hobbs

Published by the
Health for All Network
(UK) Ltd